Essential Viewpoints

The Evolution of
News Reporting

THE EVOLUTION OF

NEWS REPORTING

BY TOM ROBINSON

Content Consultant
Beverly Horvit
Adjunct Instructor
University of Missouri—Missouri School of Journalism

ABDO
Publishing Company

CREDITS

Published by ABDO Publishing Company, 8000 West 78th Street, Edina, Minnesota 55439. Copyright © 2011 by Abdo Consulting Group, Inc. International copyrights reserved in all countries. No part of this book may be reproduced in any form without written permission from the publisher. The Essential Library™ is a trademark and logo of ABDO Publishing Company.

Printed in the United States of America, North Mankato, Minnesota
052010
092010

 THIS BOOK CONTAINS AT LEAST 10% RECYCLED MATERIALS.

Editor: Chrös McDougall
Copy Editor: Paula Lewis
Interior Design and Production: Kazuko Collins
Cover Design: Kazuko Collins

Library of Congress Cataloging-in-Publication Data

Robinson, Tom.
  The evolution of news reporting / Tom Robinson.
    p. cm. — (Essential viewpoints)
  Includes bibliographical references and index.
  ISBN 978-1-61613-521-8
  1. Journalism—United States—Juvenile literature. 2. Reporters and reporting—United States—Juvenile literature. 3. Television broadcasting of news--United States—Juvenile literature. 4. Citizen journalism—United States—Juvenile literature. 5. Online journalism—United States—Juvenile literature. I. Title.
  PN4776.R55 2010
  071'.3—dc22

TABLE OF CONTENTS

Reporters from the Rocky Mountain News *hug after owners announced the paper would print its final issue the next day.*

The Financial Crunch

*N*ewsroom employees of the *Rocky Mountain News* gathered in its Denver, Colorado, office on February 26, 2009. They awaited the news they all dreaded to hear. The longtime newspaper would be printing its last issue.

Even though they guessed the announcement was forthcoming, the employees were upset. They were about to be unemployed during a time when journalism jobs were scarce. Many industries were struggling in a weak economy, and journalism was no exception. But the employees had one last mission. During their final day working for the *Rocky Mountain News*, they aimed to put out a high-quality edition. At that time, many factors—mostly financial—had made that goal nearly impossible. But together, the staff released a tribute to the nearly 150-year history of Colorado's oldest newspaper and, in a sense, an entire industry that seemed to be crumbling around them.

Editor and publisher John Temple described the mood of the staff on that last day:

> *They're very, very upset trying to process all the emotions . . . and trying to recognize that we will be putting out our final edition tomorrow. . . . It's very rare that you get to play the music at your own funeral, so you want to make sure you do it well.*[1]

The *Rocky Mountain News* printed 350,000 copies of its final edition, which included a 52-page commemorative section. The paper had lost

$16 million in 2008. The E. W. Scripps Co., which owned the newspaper, had decided to put it up for sale in December 2008. There were no buyers. A newspaper that had started in 1859 was shut down days before it would have celebrated its 150th anniversary.

Scripps vice president of newspapers Mark Contreras told *Rocky Mountain News* workers the failure was not their fault. He pointed to problems all newspapers were having. "The industry is in serious, serious trouble," Scripps chief executive officer Rich Boehne said.[2]

More Bad News

By winter of 2009, even the highest quality reporting, editing, and photography could not guarantee that modern newspapers would turn a profit. Reading habits had changed; many readers began finding their news online. This meant fewer people were buying newspapers and watching the nightly news. Fewer readers and viewers meant fewer consumers would see the advertisements in the newspapers and on television. Companies thus became less likely to buy advertising in those media.

Less than a month after the *Rocky Mountain News* closed, the *Seattle Post-Intelligencer* shut down as well. It had survived 146 years as a newspaper. The Hearst Corporation, which owned the *Seattle Post-Intelligencer*, kept a small portion of the operation alive as an online newspaper by the same name.

Around the United States, many of the largest and most famous newspaper companies were either in bankruptcy or headed toward it. Hearst was considering shutting down the *San Francisco Chronicle*, the only daily newspaper in that California city. The *Star Tribune* in Minneapolis, Minnesota, the *Daily News* and *Inquirer* in Philadelphia, Pennsylvania, the Chicago Tribune Company, and Journal Register Company are among those that filed for bankruptcy protection in 2009. The New York Times Company threatened to shut down the *Boston Globe* unless unions there made significant concessions that would cause workers to lose salaries, benefits such as health insurance, or both.

The Heart of the Controversy

Newspapers, the traditional leaders for in-depth reporting, entered the twenty-first century with shrinking circulation figures. Newspapers also began to lose classified advertising revenue to Internet alternatives. Then papers were hit with a loss of advertising in general, and matters worsened dramatically. A small number of newspapers closed down, and most of those that remained were reorganized for the future. Massive layoffs and buyouts caused newspaper staffs to shrink across the nation. One of every four newsroom jobs in 1990 no longer existed in 2008. The problem is expected to worsen due to more massive cutbacks happening at a much more rapid pace.

When companies began to cut back on advertising, major metropolitan newspapers and the companies that owned multiple midsize papers were hit hard. Fewer advertisement sales meant decreased profits for newspapers. The value of

Quality Is Not Always the Issue

The *Rocky Mountain News* was judged as a quality newspaper. The newspaper received four prestigious Pulitzer Prizes in its final decade, putting it among the national leaders in journalism.

During the week of its closing, the *Rocky Mountain News* was informed that it had been selected by the Associated Press Sports Editors for providing one of the top ten daily sports sections in the country. The Society of American Business Editors and Writers named its business section one of the best in the country.

A copy of the final issue of the Rocky Mountain News
on a counter in the newsroom

newspapers' stocks began to decrease. The loss in advertising also came in the aftermath of increases in the cost of newsprint. That combination made it increasingly difficult for newspapers and other news-based media companies to make money.

The loss of any large business is often a bad sign for the community it serves. Many people lose their jobs. It also means a service is no longer available, or consumers have fewer options. Without competition, some providers no longer face pressure to provide the highest quality.

Some consumers believe the loss of a newspaper—or any news media outlet—is more significant than the loss of other businesses. An established and once-successful newspaper such as the *Rocky Mountain News* provided more than reading material each morning. It provided a community service by monitoring the actions of government entities and keeping the public informed. As U.S. Senator Michael Bennet noted in a statement, "The *Rocky Mountain News* has chronicled the storied, and at times tumultuous, history of Colorado for nearly 150 years."[4]

Newspapers are now so understaffed they might no longer provide the same level of service as they once did. Newspaper ownership and management face the task

"Print media does much of society's heavy journalistic lifting, from flooding the zone—covering every angle of a huge story—to the daily grind of attending the City Council meeting, just in case. This coverage creates benefits even for people who aren't newspaper readers, because the work of print journalists is used by everyone from politicians to district attorneys to talk radio hosts to bloggers. The newspaper people often note that newspapers benefit society as a whole."[5]

—*Clay Shirky, adjunct professor in New York University's graduate Interactive Telecommunications Program and consultant on the social and economic effects of Internet technologies* of developing a revised business model that can effectively perform news-gathering operations while still making a profit.

Meanwhile, many scholars and media experts fear democracy will suffer with fewer professional journalists reporting on the activities of government and other powerful institutions. And, although the Internet provides free access to an abundance of information, gathering reliable information is not free. These experts argue that the quality

Wire Services and Networks

Newspapers, radio stations, and television stations receive help compiling national and international news by subscribing to a wire service or being part of a network. The Associated Press (AP) and Reuters are two prominent wire services. Most television stations gather world news from one or both of the wire services and a national network such as ABC, CBS, Fox, or NBC.

AP is a nonprofit news-gathering cooperative that provides news to its member newspapers and broadcast clients. All member media outlets are required to share their news content with AP, which it then edits and distributes. As part of the partnership with its members, the wire service often receives breaking news from them as well. Radio stations often acquire news from one of the two wire services, as do many national Web sites.

Wire services report and compile news through their own staff of journalists. Their staffs are spread across the globe and often cover beat-type content areas, such as sporting events, legislative bodies, and other scheduled functions. Local news operations, however, require a staff of local reporters, editors, and others such as still or video photographers.

of information found online in blogs and similar media is often not as high as the caliber traditionally found in print sources.

A few lawmakers have proposed ideas of government funding, or bailouts, for the news industry. Similar to 2009 legislation intended to aid the automotive industry, newspaper bailouts would give struggling companies financial assistance from the government. In exchange, however, the government would then own portions of those newspapers. Some of those concerned about protections of free speech and democracy disagree with this funding solution. They argue that government-owned news would not fairly or accurately police government agencies.

The evolution of news reporting in the face of changing technology and changing reading habits raises a number of questions. What is the role of news reporting in a democracy? Who is affected when access to professional reporting is reduced? And what effects might government bailouts have on the industry? Are new media and styles of reporting enough to replace traditional journalism—or should traditional media outlets be saved?

Seattle Post-Intelligencer

P-I: TRADITION IN TRANSITION

P-I PRESSES FALL SILENT

From print to pixels – seattlepi.com assumes venerable legacy

TUESDAY
MARCH 17, 2009
75¢
King, Kitsap, Pierce and Snohomish
counties / Thursdays 36
SEATTLEPI.COM

No ruling yet on SR 520 west-side design

Choice 'can wait' for December's impact statement

BY DEBERA CARLTON HARRELL
P-I reporter

The Legislature likely will authorize the Evergreen Point Bridge tolling and new pontoons this session but will put off deciding the freeway's west-side design – much to the dismay of many Seattle residents.

"The west side does not need to be resolved in this session ... but I think there is agreement regarding the pontoons, which are of huge concern," House Speaker Frank Chopp said in a recent interview.

Replacing the floating bridge pontoons and implementing tolling are the governor's prime concerns for the aging span, said Ron Judd, spokeswoman for Gov. Chris Gregoire.

"Here's what we're going to leave the session with: early tolling on 520 only, some further direction as to analysis of I-90 tolling, which is still in question, and early pontoon construction," he said.

Resolving design issues on the Seattle side of the bridge "can wait" until after the completion of an Environmental Impact Statement – due in December, Judd said.

But Seattle residents is the state Route 520 corridor – and Seattle Mayor Greg Nickels – worry the delay means to rewild life for Plan L, the most unpopular of the three designs forwarded to the Legislature by a state-mandated mediation team.

"We thought the Legislature was going to make a decision on the west-side design this session," said a baffled Virginia Gunby, a mediation team member who helped craft the A plan.

The mediation team, composed of volunteers, citizens, local leaders, transportation experts and others, came up with two plans, dubbed K and A, but forwarded L at the suggestion of Washington State transportation Department officials. The three are being studied in an environmental impact statement.

The K plan, supported by the broadest coalition of Seat-

"...Were it left to me to decide whether we should have a government without newspapers, or newspapers without a government, I should not hesitate a moment to prefer the latter." *Thomas Jefferson*

Seattle P-I Publisher Roger Oglesby walks past a quote by Thomas Jefferson above a P-I staircase after telling the staff that Tuesday's edition is the last.

BY DAN RICHMAN
AND ANDREA JAMES
P-I reporters

The Seattle Post-Intelligencer has printed its last edition. You're reading it.

The Hearst Corp. said Monday it would stop publishing the 146-year-old newspaper, Seattle's oldest business, and halt delivery to more than 117,600 weekday readers.

The company said, however, that it would maintain the P-I's Web site, seattlepi.com, making it the nation's largest daily newspaper to shift to an entirely digital news product.

"Tonight we'll be putting the paper to bed for the last time," Editor and Publisher Roger Oglesby told a silent newsroom Monday morning. "But the bloodline will live on."

In a news release, Hearst Chief Executive Frank Bennack Jr. said, "Our goal now is to turn seattlepi.com into the leading news and information portal in the region."

The new operation won't try to replicate the newspaper, and fewer than two dozen staffers will decide breaking news, columns from prominent Seattle residents, community databases, photo galleries, 150 citizen bloggers and links to other journalistic outlets.

About 150 other P-I employees will lose their jobs.

The landmark neon globe will remain in place atop 101 Elliott Ave. W., as the Web site will continue to be produced from offices in the

Staff members react Monday as they first get the news that today's Seattle P-I would be the paper's final edition.

Last deadline cuts like knife

For P-I staff, it's day of tears, hugs and toasts

BY LEWIS KAMB
P-I reporter

on the keyboard – emanating in the various newsrooms surrounding him –

INSIDE

WHY DID IT DIE? The JOA with the Times failed to save the P-I. **A24**

MOVE TO WEB: Journalists in

The Seattle Post-Intelligencer published its last printed edition on March 17, 2009, before switching to a smaller, online-only format.

A printing press, circa 1440

THE BIRTH OF
THE NEWS INDUSTRY

More than 2,000 years ago, Roman Emperor Julius Caesar ordered the posting of a daily sheet of events throughout Rome. Variations of a newspaper appeared in China in the eighth century. During the Renaissance period in Europe from the fourteenth through sixteenth centuries, merchants circulated handwritten newsletters with information about political and economic issues as well as stories of human interest. News pamphlets, or broadsides, appeared in Germany in the late 1400s.

In the English-speaking world, the *Oxford/ London Gazette* utilized double columns to organize text and evolved into what was considered the first true newspaper. *Publick Occurrences,* the first North American newspaper, appeared in Boston, Massachusetts, in 1690.

Forces of social change in the eighteenth century fostered the development of daily newspapers in Europe and North America. New printing technology, the growth of cities, and increased literacy all combined with the formation of new nations, nation-states, and the related philosophical discussions those creations encouraged.

Many North American newspapers came and went early in the eighteenth century. By the time the American

Early Printing

In 1440, Johannes Gutenberg drastically improved the world of printing. He invented the printing press in Germany. Instead of being written out by hand, poems, Bibles, and other books could now be printed with relative speed. The Gutenberg press paved the way for the eventual mass production of newspapers and magazines that is seen in modern times.

Revolutionary War began in 1775, all of the colonies had access to newspapers. News reporting had an especially strong presence in Massachusetts, New York, and Pennsylvania. Commentaries in newspapers from those colonies helped spread the idea of seeking independence from England and increased support for this movement. Through these media, patriots and political dissidents were able to advance their cause for democracy and a new nation.

The New Country

Newspapers were ingrained in American society from its beginnings. By the time the colonies won their independence in 1783, 43 newspapers were in print. Many more were soon launched. News reporting was built into the foundation of the Bill of Rights—the first ten amendments to the U.S. Constitution. The Bill of Rights clearly states Congress cannot control the press. The document begins:

Libel Laws

Newspapers received a major boost in the 1730s when Peter Zenger, the publisher of the *New York Weekly Journal,* successfully won a libel trial. Libel is a false or malicious published statement that damages someone's reputation. Zenger was arrested for printing allegedly libelous items about the British government. Zenger's lawyer, Andrew Hamilton, successfully argued in a 1735 trial that the items were not libelous because they were based on fact. Zenger's case served as the precedent on which U.S. libel laws are based. Libel laws now protect news organizations from being unrightfully sued.

The First Amendment to the U.S. Bill of Rights
protects the freedom of the press.

Congress shall make no law respecting an establishment of religion, or prohibiting the free exercise thereof; or abridging the freedom of speech, or of the press; or the right of the people peaceably to assemble, and to petition the Government for a redress of grievances. [1]

Including freedom of the press in the Bill of Rights assured the role of newspapers in the growing nation. Thomas Jefferson, the country's third president, once made a public statement implying

Ben Franklin Brings the News

During the eighteenth century, Founding Father Benjamin Franklin made a significant impact on the still-young North American newspaper industry. After an apprenticeship as a printer, Franklin purchased and began printing the *Pennsylvania Gazette*. He frequently wrote articles for the publication, which grew in popularity among the colonists. The paper published the colonies' first political cartoon, with Franklin as its creator. Politics and writing would often cross paths in Franklin's life. He eventually became one of the drafters of the Declaration of Independence.

that newspapers were more important to the country than government itself. "Were it left to me to decide whether we should have a government without newspapers or newspapers without a government, I should not hesitate a moment to prefer the latter," Jefferson said.[2]

In the country's early days, newspapers were somewhat of a luxury item for the wealthy. Newspaper subscriptions were usually paid for in advance and unaffordable to the working class. Technological advances made printing presses and paper less expensive. In the 1830s, newspapers could be sold for a penny a copy, leading the business to be referred to as the "Penny Press." More and more Americans were now able to read, and newspapers helped stimulate their developing literacy skills.

Newspapers allowed many Americans to follow the developments of the Civil War (1861–1865). Reporters transmitted information from the battlefields by telegraph, so the news was available

more quickly than ever. In the
decades following the Civil War,
the Industrial Revolution created
larger, faster printing presses that
could print up to 10,000 copies
or sheets in an hour. Soon, papers
were including illustrations and, by
the 1880s, photographs. The success
of newspapers increased: according
to U.S. census figures, the number
of newspapers being printed in the
country grew from 2,526 in 1850 to
11,314 in 1880.

First Daily

The *Pennsylvania Packet and General Advertiser* became the first daily newspaper in the United States. John Dunlap and David C. Claypoole published the newspaper, which became a daily paper on September 21, 1784.

Industry Changes

At the close of the nineteenth century, industry leaders Joseph Pulitzer and William Randolph Hearst had pushed newspapers much closer to the medium recognized today. Before that time, specific political parties often supported newspapers. Pulitzer and Hearst moved their publications away from political affiliations and toward the notion of independent reporting. However, both men strove for large profits, large headlines, and large circulations. The competition between them resulted in what came to be known as yellow journalism. Exaggerated articles led to greater sales. But the inaccuracies of the reporting style eventually raised reader awareness of what unbiased news reporting really was. The accuracy of their publications' reporting was called into question after their coverage of the sinking of the USS *Maine* was noted to be sensationalist. The sinking was one of the incidents that led to the Spanish-American War (1898–1901). But some historians note that the inflated and overly dramatized

Broadcast News

Radio news was just beginning to emerge when Edward R. Murrow headed to Europe to report on World War II. The first regular broadcast of daily news began with Murrow's *The World Today* program on CBS radio. Beginning in late 1940, the program stayed on the air until 1946.

The CBS-TV News began broadcasting in 1948 with Douglas Edwards as news anchor. Walter Cronkite took over as anchor in 1962 and remained on the job until 1981, when Dan Rather replaced him. Cronkite built a giant reputation. He became known as the "most trusted man in America." In one of the most famous moments in television news history, Cronkite broke the news to the American public that President John F. Kennedy had died of gunshot wounds.

The *CBS Evening News* expanded from 15 to 30 minutes in 1963. Within four years, both NBC and ABC also had half-hour nightly news programs. NBC began *Today*, a morning show, on January 14, 1952. CBS started *60 Minutes*, its weekly news magazine show, in 1968.

In 1980, Ted Turner created the Cable News Network (CNN). It became the first network to broadcast news 24 hours a day, seven days a week. Today, CNN competes with numerous other cable channels, including Fox News Channel and MSNBC.

headlines also strongly contributed to swaying public opinion.

By 1900, the modern newspaper had essentially developed with photos, comics, and sports sections. Over the decades that followed, advertising revenues grew, and many publicly owned corporations began buying newspaper companies from the families that owned them. For example, in 1969, Walter Annenberg sold the *Philadelphia Inquirer* to the Knight newspaper chain. The Knight chain went on to become Knight Ridder before being bought by The McClatchy Company.

Corporate involvement increased the creation of newspaper chains and added pressure to produce more profits for stock market investors. Those pressures led to some small cuts in staffing, and some operations were consolidated.

DECLINING VALUE

Share prices on Wall Street provide a good indication of the troubles the newspaper industry has faced. According to a report in the *New Yorker*, media entrepreneur Alan Mutter said independent, publicly traded American newspapers lost 42 percent of their market value from 2005 to 2008.

The same report, published on March 31, 2008, notes that McClatchy lost 80 percent of its stock value. Lee Enterprises, another newspaper chain, lost 75 percent of its value. The losses by McClatchy and Lee are notable because each had made major investments by buying out other failing newspaper chains. McClatchy bought up the bulk of the Knight Ridder chain while Lee bought out Pulitzer. That left each company with debt, which became harder to pay off as the newspapers made less and less profit. Even the *New York Times,* one of the most respected newspapers in the country, saw a decrease of 54 percent in its stock value from the end of 2004 through early 2008.

Such decreases represented a major shift in the history of newspapers. As Eric Alterman wrote for the *New Yorker*:

> Until recently, newspapers were accustomed to operating as high-margin monopolies. To own the dominant, or only, newspaper in a mid-sized American city was, for many decades, a kind of license to print money.[3]

Many industries, including newspapers, evolved during the Industrial Revolution.

Competition from the Internet might prove to be insurmountable for print newspapers.

THE IMPACT OF
THE INTERNET

Throughout the twentieth century, newspapers competed with radio, then television, and eventually the Internet, to be the most trusted news source. Nightly news television shows had the advantage of using video to help tell a story. Radio stations were able to provide the most immediate updates thanks to listeners' ease of access and the stations' ability to report live broadcasts. Many Americans caught hourly radio updates while driving. What both of these broadcast options lacked in depth—particularly radio, which usually had smaller staffs and budgets—newspapers provided.

In the heyday of mid-twentieth century newspapers, a daily newspaper would publish two editions. One would be available in the early morning, and the other would release in the afternoon. Readership of afternoon newspapers eventually began to shrink. Many of the afternoon newspapers struggled to compete against television newscasts, which aired in the evening. Also, delivering the product to people's doorsteps on time proved difficult through afternoon traffic. Morning newspapers continued to thrive in most markets. Many people read them with breakfast or picked them up on the way to work as their primary source for news. Each newspaper offered a wide range of reports, featuring in-depth looks at the biggest stories from international news, local news, and sports.

With the support of advertising, many news outlets were able to adjust and stay prominent as technology and lifestyles changed. The arrival of the Internet, however, offered the biggest challenge yet.

News Available 24/7

When Cable News Network (CNN) was launched in 1980, it began to change how news was broadcast on television. CNN became the first television station to broadcast news around the clock. Other news networks soon emerged, such as the Fox News Channel and MSNBC. These networks were able to provide immediate saturation coverage of major news and breaking stories.

News coverage became even more accessible as the Internet experienced an early stretch of exponential growth at the close of the twentieth century. A story written for a newspaper was limited in many ways. It had to be written and designed to fit the allotted space in the newspaper, printed, and then delivered before the customer could read it. Those constraints did not apply to the Internet. With less time needed to post the stories online, news outlets could publish breaking news much sooner. Also, events could be continually updated, whereas a printed newspaper could not provide additional information until the next edition of the paper. The Internet also allowed people to read online editions of newspapers from all around the world.

The broadcast and print news organizations were forced to react to new competition. Some newspaper editors wanted to emphasize quality reporting. They tried to produce more investigative and analytical pieces to offset the loss of immediate breaking news. Others sought ways to use the Internet to their advantage. However, the results showed that adjusting to the new reality was not that simple.

Development of the Internet

In 1967, the Advanced Research Projects Agency (ARPA) contracted with the Stanford Research Institute to complete a project for the U.S. military. The two groups were to design a system the military could use to share information between computers over great distances. The system evolved into one that was also used by researchers at colleges who were exchanging data. Today, it has become the Internet.

The first messages were exchanged in 1969 between a computer at the University of California, Los Angeles, and the Stanford Research Institute in Menlo Park, California. E-mail messages began being transmitted two years later.

When Netscape released the first commercially available Web browser late in 1994, surfing the Internet became an option for the public. Businesses, including news-gathering operations, began building Web sites in an attempt to draw Internet surfers to their products. The invention of Web browsers to easily maneuver throughout the World Wide Web led to rapid expansion of the Internet. In 1993, there were an estimated 130,000 Web pages on the Internet. By 1998, that number had increased to more than 30 million.

Twenty-four hour cable news channels such as CNN allow breaking news to air immediately.

Newspaper companies went through a cycle of layoffs, bankruptcies, and some closings in the first decade of the twenty-first century. Ironically, Pulitzer Prize-winning *Washington Post* columnist Eugene Robinson used the Internet to explain the demise of the industry. In an online chat session with the paper's readers, Robinson wrote:

> *Family ownership gave way to chain ownership. Afternoon papers went into decline and began to fail, leaving many cities with one-paper monopolies. These newspapers made*

big profits—margins of 20 percent or more were pretty common—as chains squeezed them for every last drop. Newspapers didn't understand how the Internet would change the world. First radio and then television failed to kill newspapers (as had been predicted), but this is a more serious challenge.[1]

Newspapers struggled to compete with the vast amount of information available on the Internet. However, as Robinson noted, the increase of available information did not translate into an increase in reporting.

During a 2007 lecture in London, England, *New York Times* executive editor Bill Keller said reliable news reporting was lacking—despite the increasing amount of content available online and on television. Keller said Internet searches, blogs, social networking Web sites, and television commentary come up short of replacing what news reporting provides. "That may sound like a strange thing to say in the age of too much information," Keller said. "The civic labor performed by journalists on the ground cannot be replicated by legions of bloggers hunched over their computer screens."[2]

ADVANTAGES OF INTERNET NEWS

Others see the new forms of information on the Internet as different, but not necessarily inferior, ways of spreading information. Blogs and Web sites not affiliated with major news organizations have helped tell stories. Blogs (or Weblogs) are Web sites in which a series of entries are written about a particular topic. The information can be original written material from the blogger. However, blogs often feature short introductions to news items from other Web sites or sources and provide links back to those stories. A blog offers a simple and effective way for the author to offer commentary to other works. The blogger is able to post a link and then make comments in the same area. Although some bloggers have journalistic training or topic expertise and produce reliable reports based on information they have gathered, many offer commentary and information that has not been verified.

Some blogs have broken major news stories. The Drudge Report blog is credited with breaking the news of President Bill Clinton's relationship with White House intern Monica Lewinsky in 1998. Mississippi's Trent Lott lost power in the U.S. Senate and eventually resigned after bloggers

President Bill Clinton met Monica Lewinsky in 1995.
The Drudge Report blog became the first
source to report on their affair years later in 1998.

reported remarks he made in a speech that favored segregation—remarks that had not been reported by other media. Blogs helped discredit documents Dan Rather of CBS used for a 2004 report on *60 Minutes* about President George W. Bush's service in the National Guard. In 2007, the Talking Points Memo blog helped spread the word when politics contributed to the firing of U.S. attorneys around the country. U.S. attorneys prosecute federal crimes in the regions they serve. Nominated by the president and confirmed by the Senate, they are rarely fired.

From the September 11, 2001, terrorist attacks to the 2010 earthquake in Haiti, the Internet has helped to quickly spread news of major disasters. In the aftermath of Hurricane Katrina in 2006, the *New Orleans Times–Picayune* could not always keep its presses running and its delivery trucks on the road. The blog that the *Times–Picayune* produced won a Pulitzer Prize for Public Service.

Political Blogs

Many blogs are used for political purposes. Liberal-leaning blogs were originally more prominent, but blogs supporting virtually every political viewpoint have emerged.

The quality of online information continues to concern many editors, though. *New York Times* executive editor Bill Keller once referred to the growing number of information options available to the public as a "media tsunami." Keller argued that all the options could not combine to substitute for the value of reporting.

During his speech, he said of news reporting:

It cannot be replaced by a search engine. It cannot be supplanted by shouting heads or satirical television shows.

What is absent from the vast array of new media outlets is, first and foremost, the great engine of newsgathering— the people who witness events, ferret out information, supply context and explanation.[3]

PRIMARY SOURCE FOR NEWS

As a source of national and international news, the Internet passed newspapers for the first time in December 2008, according to the *News Interest Index*, a weekly survey conducted by the Pew Research Center for the People & the Press. However, the Associated Press reports much of the news that appears in online portals, such as Yahoo. The Associated Press also supplies most of the national and international news to most daily newspapers and their Web sites.

As of December 23, 2008, only television was a more commonly used

News for the Under-30 Crowd

In 2007 and 2008, the use of the Internet as a news source rose dramatically among people younger than 30. On December 23, 2008, the *News Interest Index* indicated an increase from 34 percent in September 2007 to 59 percent in December 2008 of the number of younger Americans who said they get most of their national and international news online. Fifty-nine percent of those in the same age group also said television was their source for that news. The numbers do not contradict each other, as people were allowed to give multiple responses to the survey.

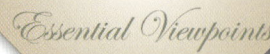

news source than the Internet. At that point, 40 percent of respondents to the Pew Research Center's weekly survey agreed that they received "much" of their national and international news from the Internet. Seventy percent of respondents said the same regarding television; only 35 percent did for newspapers.

As of December 2008, more people receive their national and international news from the Internet than from newspapers.

The Philadelphia Inquirer *newsroom has many different sections that help deliver the news both in print and online.*

STRUGGLES WITH
TECHNOLOGY AND
COPYRIGHT

reating a new newspaper is a major challenge for any publisher. Running a newspaper is expensive. Among the costs are staff salaries; supplies such as ink, paper, and one or more printing presses; and the infrastructure needed for distribution. Furthermore, the newspaper would need to establish name recognition and a positive reputation. Yet, for years, newspapers were so profitable that many entrepreneurs were willing to overcome these obstacles and create their own editions.

Today, creating a new Web site or blog has proven much easier and much less expensive. The costs of buying a domain name and online hosting are dwarfed in comparison to the costs of running a newspaper. Many sites exist today that allow users to publish stories for free. Newspapers generally still have the advantage of name recognition and reputations as being credible sources. However, as fewer people are reading newspapers and fewer businesses are advertising in them, newspaper profits are falling. Today, owning a large metropolitan newspaper is rarely considered a profitable business venture.

In the past, many businesses were accustomed to paying for newspaper advertisements. Newspapers reached a wide audience and engaged readers. That made newspaper advertising more effective than stand-alone advertising material such as flyers, which could be ignored as junk mail. But as use of the

Internet began to change reading habits, particularly among younger people, newspapers were forced to look for a new business model.

Lost Revenue Streams

Many newspaper owners anticipated they would have to adjust to the Internet era, as they had with radio and television competition. However, determining what changes to make while remaining profitable has proven to be a challenge. The entire news-gathering industry, but particularly those on the newspaper side, has been evolving in an ever-changing technological environment.

A common response from newspapers was to use the Internet and the print medium together.

Fighting the Fans

Dave Barry's popular humor column in the *Miami Herald* led to a series of books and a television show based on some of his writings. The Knight Ridder newspaper chain syndicated Barry's columns. That means Knight Ridder sold the rights to reprint the columns to other newspapers around the country.

In 1993, Knight Ridder began an investigation into the unauthorized distribution of Barry's columns through the newly developing Internet. The chain found mailing lists that forwarded the columns. Knight Ridder learned that a Midwestern teenager who was a Barry fan was one of the people responsible for unauthorized distribution of Barry's columns. In the years ahead, newspaper executives debated whether it was wise to battle with people who enjoyed their articles and were trying to encourage others to do the same.

This was intended to keep the established business thriving while grabbing on to a piece of the emerging media market.

Classified advertising filled newspaper pages, often comprising its own section. The material was almost entirely paid for by the people who submitted items. Along with traditional advertising revenue, newspapers lost significant classified ad revenue to the Internet. The Internet began offering many alternatives for people seeking job listings and selling various items. Craigslist.com hit newspapers particularly hard. Craigslist offers the same service as newspaper classifieds, but for free. It also has a much larger potential audience and features easy searchability.

Clay Shirky, an adjunct professor in New York University's graduate Interactive Telecommunications Program, writes, consults, and teaches about the economic effects of Internet technologies. Shirky looks back on the reactions of newspaper owners to the Internet as inadequate and uncreative. In the 1990s, while attempts were being made to preserve the existing news-gathering operations, the Internet continued to grow. It became impossible for any one industry to control

Classified ads helped newspapers make big profits for many years.

the way information was distributed. Shirky believes the answer for how newspapers could survive might be elusive because it might not exist. "Nothing will work," he wrote. "There is no general model for newspapers to replace the one the Internet just broke."[1]

In an extreme interpretation, what advances the printing press helped start more than five centuries earlier, the Internet is threatening to bring to an end. Shirky states:

It makes increasingly less sense even to talk about a publishing industry, because the core problem publishing solves—the incredible difficulty, complexity, and expense of making something available to the public—has stopped being a problem.[2]

In a 2009 blog entry, he wrote in detail about the various theories of how to profitably blend newspapers into the Internet era and why each of them failed. The attempts and the reasons for their failure included partnering with specific search companies such as America Online, or AOL. As search engines have improved, the option to have news content available on a sole site became irrelevant. Also, news Web sites built to be supported by advertising failed to produce the same profits as print ads. Charging readers for small amounts of content had mixed results. This was intended to be similar to buying a newspaper at a store or paying to download music. However, newspaper content is not the same as songs on iTunes. The online music store has thrived with micropayments. But unlike a song or an album, many variations of the same news story are available. According to Shirky, newspapers also risked alienating readers as the companies attempted to use copyright laws to keep people from freely distributing reported information.

Copyright and the News Online

Opponents to Shirky would argue that, although posting information on the Internet is inexpensive, the cost of gathering information—reporting on events and issues everywhere from Washington to Afghanistan, for example—is not. Seasoned journalists argue that the news does not report itself. Content must be researched, gathered, created, edited, and vetted. And because that content comes with creative costs, many newspapers are also willing to pay to protect the copyright to it. Copyright infringement, or actively using published material without the owner's permission, has become widespread as the Internet and other electronic media have grown.

Newspapers have tried to maintain control over their copyrighted materials in a number of ways, including the use of hardware and software that limits information sharing. But limiting customers from copying information from the Web has turned some customers away. Additionally, aggressive lawsuits against copyright infringers have done little to slow the use of material from newspapers. These lawsuits were intended to make an example of those who infringed on a copyright and discourage future abuses. But given the anonymity of the Internet and the widespread repurposing of information, the litigation is extremely inadequate.

Despite Shirky's concerns, the Associated Press has decided to begin monitoring how its content is used online. "We can no longer stand by and watch others walk off with our work under misguided legal theories," said Dean Singleton, chairman of the Associated Press Board of Directors, at the 2009 annual meeting.[3] The *Wall Street Journal* has had success charging for some access to online content, and the *New York Times* has also announced plans to charge for unlimited access to its online content.

Top News Sites

The top five news Web sites, as of July 2009, according to ebizmedia. com:

1. cnn.com: affiliated with the cable television news network
2. yahoo.news: Web-only site that combines original content with news from other sources
3. digg.com: a news-aggregating site where readers help choose the top stories from other sources
4. nytimes.com: site affiliated with the major newspaper
5. usatoday.com: site affiliated with the national newspaper

Readers Have Their Say

Many news sites, in an attempt to engage their Web audience, have allowed readers to add comments below stories. This process has led to debates about censorship and good taste. If the sites do not monitor or control the comments, readers might add questionable or unproven material that would have never been included by a reporter.

Generally, online content providers are protected from libel suits over comments posted by outside parties. News reports on controversial subjects have, at times, led to distasteful remarks being added in the comments section below the story.

One drawback to monitoring the comment is that it requires staffing. Also, monitors have to exercise good judgment. Overly strict monitors might deter future interaction.

Crossing Media

Newspapers, magazines, and broadcast news operations have, in general, failed to produce a profit from their Internet operations. That does not mean these ventures have been a failure. Many outlets have created Web sites that have generated interest among existing and new readers.

In many cases, television stations used the Web to add written stories. Likewise, newspapers eventually added sound and video to their online articles. On the simplest levels, the different media entered into each other's areas of expertise. This provided another challenge for those already struggling news outlets.

As online news sites continue to improve, fewer people are still subscribing to home delivery of a newspaper.

News of Michael Jackson's sudden death shocked the world in 2009.

THE NEWS OF TODAY

*P*op music superstar Michael Jackson passed away on June 25, 2009. When Jackson was rushed to a Los Angeles, California, hospital that day, the modern methods of news coverage were put on display.

TMZ, an entertainment news Web site, was the first to report Jackson's death. It did so well ahead of television news operations and newspaper Web sites. From TMZ's reporting, the news that the singer was dead spread over social networking Web sites such as Twitter and Facebook. Twitter is a Web site that allows users to post short updates. The updates are often linked to news items or personal reactions. Meanwhile, television reports still cautiously stated Jackson was hospitalized. Per journalistic standards, the television stations were seeking confirmation of his death. The individuals who post to social networking sites such as Twitter and Facebook do not need to take such steps, so at times they are wrong.

The Scene

Paramedics were sent to Jackson's house after a 911 call just after noon on June 25. Within an hour, TMZ reported Jackson was in cardiac arrest. At 2:44 p.m., TMZ reported his death. Other news outlets later confirmed Jackson had officially been listed as dead at 2:26 p.m.

When the *Los Angeles Times* reported Jackson's death on its Web site at 2:51 p.m., many other news sources credited the newspaper with the report of the death while seeking their own confirmations. Time Warner owns both CNN and TMZ. However, CNN did not report its own confirmation until 4:25 p.m., when the official announcement was made by the coroner's office.

TMZ's managing editor, Harvey Levin, did not seem surprised that other news outlets refused to acknowledge his organization's reports. "That's typical," Levin said. "No matter what they say, people know we broke the story. That's how competitors handle it. There is no issue about our credibility."[1]

Where to Look

Some Internet users responded to word of Jackson's death on Twitter, Facebook, TMZ, and other sources by turning on their televisions. There, they found news anchors still waiting to report the death as a fact. However, the search for further confirmation online was also delayed. On June 25, from 2:40 to 3:15 p.m., the traffic was so high on Google.com that some users were unable to receive responses to searches about Michael Jackson.

Levin also noted: "We were getting calls from everyone under the sun, established news operations, asking, 'Are you sure?' . . . That's such an odd question. We would not have published it if it were not true."[2] The traditional news outlets were clearly hesitant to report news from the TMZ Web site as fact. TMZ and other emerging Web sites have struggled to be taken seriously by the more

Some traditional news outlets were hesitant to publish TMZ's report that Michael Jackson had died.

established organizations. A CNN spokesman told the *Los Angeles Times* that the news network exercised caution because of the nature of the story.

The public responded to early reports and spread the word through social Web sites. On that day, Twitter was processing more than 5,000 Jackson messages a minute at one point, causing technical difficulties for the Web site.

WHEN DOES NEWS BECOME NEWS?

TMZ's early reports of Jackson's death might have been ignored by other news organizations

Engaging the Reader

A search engine such as Yahoo! or Google can lead a viewer to a Web site. After that, it is up to that Web site to keep the viewer interested, according to Marissa Mayer, vice president of Search Products and User Experience for Google. "When a reader finishes an article online, it is the publication's responsibility to answer the reader who asks, 'What should I do next?'" Mayer said. "Much like Amazon.com suggests related products and YouTube makes it easy to play another video, publications should provide obvious and engaging next steps for users. Today, there are still many publications that don't fully take advantage of the numerous tools that keep readers engaged and on their site."[3]

because the reports were based on information from unnamed sources. Other organizations have used unnamed sources when they believe the sources to be appropriate. However, most organizations try to avoid this practice as much as possible. When a less-established news operation uses an unnamed source, the established operations are more likely to question the report.

As technology evolves, there are increasingly more ways for news to be spread. However, that does not mean all of the sources are credible or that they practice proper journalism. Most traditional news outlets have certain standards of reporting that must be met before publishing a story. For example, a reporter for a major newspaper is usually required to confirm the details of a story with reliable sources. Unless they have a compelling reason to protect a source's identity, reporters usually name their sources in the story. Most U.S. newspapers also strive to be objective. That means the reporter usually tries to obtain a wide range of sources that represent all sides of a story before publishing it. By upholding these standards for many years, journalists have earned the trust of the public.

Newer forms of news gathering, such as blogging or sharing information on a social networking site, often lack these journalism standards. This concerns some people, in part,

An Unintended Change

Newspapers do not post solely their own content on the Internet. They also provide items from independent Web sites. In the process, however, newspapers have been accused of doing just what they often criticize blogs for: offering too much commentary without the original reporting to back it up.

Scott Spjut of Demockracy.com, an online political magazine, noted that the pressure from Internet media has forced newspaper Web sites away from the print product's main goal—namely, publishing the news of the previous day. "They had to have breaking news, updates, and online-only stories. . . . But the demand for unique content was greater than what could be supplied. [So they] put anything they could on their site, including speculation, editorial, and gossip. More and more reporters were expected to also be bloggers—not just focusing on the facts, but ranting about them as well."[4]

Journalistic balance, something newspapers and television stations frequently take pride in, can get lost in the process. "As a news organization produces more and more opinion and editorial, it will naturally drift toward a certain ideology," Spjut said. "This creates liberal or conservative networks or papers—instead of objective news."[5]

Traditional Roles

Generally speaking, the roles of reporter and columnist have been distinct throughout newspaper history. Reporters generally write fact-based stories by obtaining information from all sides of an issue or event. Columnists offer their personal opinions on issues and events.

Some newspapers allow reporters to also write columns, as long as they are clearly labeled as such. Others believe it is important for reporters to avoid writing columns on issues they cover. The editorial page often contains commentary, or editorials, that reflect the newspaper management's positions on issues. The editorial page often allows a limited number of commentaries from the readers as well.

because these newer outlets do not have long reputations of being fair and accurate. A small blog has less to lose by being inaccurate than the *New York Times*, for example. An individual or a company suing the *New York Times* for libel has more to gain financially and publicly in recompense, whereas a lawsuit against a small blog that has few, if any, resources would not result in significant compensation. Many bloggers do not have journalism backgrounds and do not always understand the methods necessary to confirm a report. Even more important, many bloggers do not strive to be objective. Their intent is to post either commentaries to a news item or to push their own points of view.

David Simon is a former reporter who worked for the *Baltimore Sun* from 1982 to 1995. He is also the creator of the HBO television series *The Wire*. In a prepared speech, Simon explained his concerns about declining quality in journalism before a subcommittee of the Senate Commerce Committee during a 2009 Hearing on the Future of Journalism:

> From those speaking on behalf of new media, Weblogs, and that which goes twitter, you will be treated to assurances that American journalism has a perfectly fine future online, and that a great democratization in newsgathering is taking place . . . . High-end journalism is dying in America and, unless a new economic model is achieved, it will not be reborn on the Web or anywhere else. The Internet is a marvelous tool and clearly it is the informational delivery system of our future, but thus far it does not deliver much first-generation reporting. Instead, it leeches that reporting from mainstream news publications, whereupon aggregating Web sites and bloggers contribute little more than repetition, commentary, and froth.[6]

Simon said readers are led to Web sites that compile the news and away from the newspapers that actually produce the work. "In short, the parasite is slowly killing the host," he said.[7]

Simon pointed out advantages and disadvantages in the additional voices that are available on the Internet. "It is nice that more people can have their say in new media," he said. "And while some of our Internet commentary is . . . rampantly ideological, ridiculously inaccurate, and occasionally juvenile, some of it is also quite good, even original."[8]

A New Attempt

There is much debate over whether certain new models can work as replacements for established news organizations. With diminishing advertising support for newspapers, however, other options have to be sought.

One example of a new model in news is Voiceofsandiego.org, which offers daily updates on news and opinion from San Diego, California. The site relies on donations and trust funds to exist in its nonprofit form. It features a professional staff that has won several journalism awards. The site also offers readers in San Diego an alternative to the *Union-Tribune* newspaper. Voiceofsandiego.org has received enough support to exist and succeed as an online-only news source.

Slashing Income

Some publishers are considering a switch to online-only newspapers as a way to save money. Newspapers can cut the costs of printing and distributing the paper while making staffing cuts for jobs that are no longer needed in the operation, such as layout designers. Such decisions, however, run the risk of eliminating revenue at a higher rate than expenses. Advertising rates are lower and much less stable online. There is also no commonly agreed-upon solution to replace the money brought in from newspaper sales.

Many new news formats are abandoning a printed product.

Washington Post *reporters Carl Bernstein,* left, *and Bob Woodward,* right, *uncovered the Watergate scandal in the early 1970s.*

MEDIA AS A WATCHDOG

An active and unhampered media is woven into the fabric of a democracy. This has particularly been true throughout the history of the United States. Reports in early colonial newspapers helped build support for the revolution that formed the country. Over the centuries, news coverage has been wide-ranging, addressing everything from deaths and marriages to crime and social problems. Newspapers, and later, television reporters, brought Americans information about progress in foreign wars. News agencies also monitored political developments, including elections.

The media as a whole has impacted public policy by carrying out two roles. First, the media helps keep the public informed. Its very presence has also served as a reminder for people not to break the rules. The classic example of media impacting the country is the Watergate scandal in the early 1970s. *Washington Post* reporters Bob Woodward and Carl Bernstein wrote a series of investigative stories that tied break-ins at the Watergate Hotel to questionable activities at the White House during Richard Nixon's presidency. At a minimum, the stories by Woodward and Bernstein kept the issue in the news and gave

What's in a Name?

Watergate, the political scandal that led to Richard Nixon's resignation as president of the United States, takes its name from the site where the story developed. In 1972, five men were arrested after breaking into the Democratic National Committee offices at the Watergate Hotel in Washington DC. The *Washington Post* reported that those men were close to Nixon.

the Federal Bureau of Investigation (FBI) reason to continue digging. Some scholars argue the stories did much more. The corruption uncovered by the FBI and reported by the *Washington Post* led to Nixon becoming the only U.S. president to resign from office.

Staff and budget cuts within media organizations, particularly within the newspaper industry, mean that fewer reporters are actively monitoring local and national entities. If the trend continues, even fewer journalists might soon be covering local beats. Interesting and entertaining stories might be missed. But more importantly, the media's vital role as watchdog could be in jeopardy. Without reporters monitoring them, future politicians and others who serve the public might be tempted to break the rules or perform lower quality work because no one will be monitoring them.

In a democracy, news media ideally is independent and provides diverse viewpoints. Scholars argue that media needs to be free from government control and pressures from private interests that could limit the ability to report for the public. When the information produced by news organizations maintains credibility and remains

Former Baltimore Sun *reporter David Simon said today's newspapers do not thoroughly cover their communities.*

free from influence, an informed public is better prepared to make educated decisions.

Who Is Watching?

Journalism is sometimes called a "watchdog." In other words, reporters hold government and businesses accountable for their actions. "The goal of watchdog journalism is to see that people in power provide information the public should have," according to Barry Sussman of the Nieman Foundation for Journalism at Harvard University.[1]

Investigative journalism has been a hallmark of watchdog journalism. It seeks to expose abuses of justice, malpractice, and other controversies through extensive inquiry and research. Many media outlets have maintained forms of investigative journalism—even in times of cutbacks. Some blogs and Web sites have also been able to do so. However, many wonder if investigative reporting on blogs can be impartial.

Investigative reporting today is not always as timely as it has been. Many investigative stories are now preplanned series that look deeply into an already identified issue. Previously, the result of grassroots work by reporters would point out the need for an in-depth analysis of an issue that was not yet on the public's radar.

Former *Baltimore Sun* reporter David Simon blames newspaper management for seeking awards and attention rather than consistent, thorough coverage. At the 2009 Senate hearing, he said editors:

pursue a handful of special projects. Pulitzer-sniffing as one does. The self-gratification of my profession does not come, you see, from covering a city and covering it well, from explaining an increasingly complex and interconnected world to citizens, from holding basic institutions accountable on a daily basis. It comes from someone handing you a plaque and taking your picture.[4]

Simon said readers care more about having their communities thoroughly covered than they do about the newspaper's awards for high-profile stories. Like many others, Simon bemoans the loss of local reporting that has resulted from

Watergate

An independent, active, and powerful press allowed *Washington Post* reporters Bob Woodward and Carl Bernstein the resources and the freedom to link Richard Nixon to the Watergate scandal. When other media shied away from the story, Woodward and Bernstein kept digging with the help of a key anonymous source.

Although readers might appreciate in-depth coverage of their local issues, some analysts believe there have been negative effects for the national media in the aftermath of Watergate. Nixon supporters accused reporters of being overzealous or "out to get" the president. Others believe the pursuit of Watergate-type stories has led reporters to search for unfounded conspiracies.

"[Watergate] created a model of journalism that is easily abused and debased," Columbia University historian Alan Brinkley stated. It also:

created generations of people trying to replicate that role by digging in more and more unsavory ways. As much as Watergate is a model of the journalism that we admire, you can also see it in the origins of the distrust we have today.[5]

Good Work

Enterprising journalists can still find ways to hold government accountable. *The Bristol* (Virginia) *Herald Courier*, with a circulation of about 40,000, won the 2010 Pulitzer Prize for Public Service for the work of Daniel Gilbert. He uncovered the mismanagement of natural-gas royalties that were owed to thousands of people. That prompted action from state lawmakers. Gilbert was able to find his information by assembling a database based on material uncovered through the Freedom of Information Act, and he ultimately helped hold a state agency accountable.

Internet competition. He said bloggers and citizen journalists are not putting in the time working the courthouses, city hall, or places where police officers gather. They are not as familiar with the local issues and players. That lack of contact makes it more difficult for them to raise questions that hold those in power accountable.

At the Senate Hearing on the Future of Journalism, former *Washington Post* managing editor Steve Coll said journalism's role in society may be dramatized through coverage of the Vietnam War, Watergate, or terrorism, but work on lower levels should not be forgotten. He stated:

Arguably, it was through the less visible role of independent reporting at the local and state levels—the constant and increasingly sophisticated watch-dogging of local school boards, zoning boards, mayors, and state legislatures—that the postwar era of professional journalism made its greatest contributions.[6]

A series of reports in the Washington Post *uncovered a scandal that led to President Richard Nixon's resignation in 1974.*

In January 2009, Twitter helped spread the news that a US Airways plane had crashed into the Hudson River in New York.

A DIFFERENT STYLE

On January 15, 2009, a US Airways airplane crashed into the Hudson River between Manhattan and northern New Jersey. Freelance writer Eric Zeman first found out about the crash via Twitter. Zeman first went to Web sites affiliated with cable news operations (CNN.com and FoxNews.com) and a major newspaper (NYTimes.com) but found that information about the crash was not yet available. He turned on his television. WNBC Channel 4, which services the New York City area, was just beginning to interrupt programming with local news reports about the crash.

The Twitter.com Web site was created in 2006 and is self-described as "a free service that lets you keep in touch with people through the exchange of quick, frequent answers to one simple question: What are you doing?"[1] Twitter members can use their cell phones to send brief messages, known as Tweets, which are then posted on Twitter. Depending on the user's preferences, the messages are forwarded to his or her "followers." Twitter can be seemingly meaningless chatter when used to describe the mundane developments of one's day. However, on this day, it was much more. Many Twitter users followed the developments of this major news story and forwarded the information to their followers.

"If you aren't familiar with Twitter, it is one of those things, like MySpace, that sounds totally ridiculous and stupid when you first hear about it. But once you start using it, you realize how much fun it is."[2]

—*Eric Nuzum, author of* The Dead Travel Fast

Twitter allows people to share short messages with an online community.

Many of these followers then forwarded again in a continuous cycle. Zeman was able to follow the early developments at the crash scene by using Twitter.

Zeman wrote on his Information Week blog:

> *Today was yet another indicator that Twitter is the way we're going to consume breaking news in the future. . . . Within minutes there were hundreds of Tweets about the crash, complete with pictures from eyewitnesses and even one person who was on a NYC ferry headed to the crash site to pick up passengers. That's amazing power, all thanks to the mobile phone and a social networking tool called Twitter. News spreads like wildfire when you can tell 100, 500, 1,000 people at once with a single Tweet.[3]*

Not everyone shared Zeman's enthusiasm. He referred to Twitter as the "power of people to communicate events in an instant."[4] The immediate access to unfiltered eyewitness reports was indeed unprecedented. However, critics balance this advantage with a reminder that the informal reporting was being done by those who did not have the same standards of accuracy as journalists. Depending on the person the reader is "following"—a professional journalist, a friend, someone unknown to them—judging the authenticity and accuracy of a particular Tweet might be difficult.

One usage of Twitter is to direct users to a news article written by a professional journalist. However, Twitter can also be used to spread unconfirmed, incomplete, or inaccurate information.

New Sources

Zeman expects to see more news breaking on Twitter. Others look to blogs and various forms of citizen

Most "Followed" Twitter Accounts

According to Twitterholic.com in April 2010, the ten most followed Twitter accounts are:

1. Ashton Kutcher (aplusk)
2. Britney Spears (britneyspears)
3. Ellen DeGeneres (TheEllenShow)
4. Barack Obama (BarackObama)
5. Lady Gaga (ladygaga)
6. Oprah Winfrey (oprah)
7. Kim Kardashian (KimKardashian)
8. John Mayer (johncmayer)
9. Twitter (twitter)
10. Ryan Seacrest (ryanseacrest)[5]

journalists to get information. Citizen journalists are not trained journalists but write about what is going on in their town. Blogs often have a base of professional reporting with the commenter referring and linking to an original piece of traditional journalism.

Most Popular Blogs

According to ebizmedia.com, the most popular blogs as of July 2009 were:
1. tmz.com (entertainment news)
2. gizmodo.com (gadgets and technology)
3. perezhilton.com (celebrity gossip)
4. engadget.com (technology)
5. boingboing.net (gadgets and technology)
6. techcrunch.com (reviews of new Internet products and technology)
7. lifehacker.com (computer tips, shortcuts, and downloads)
8. gawker.com (entertainment, news, and media)
9. fanhouse.com (sports)
10. autoblog.com (automobile industry)[6]

These alternatives place some added responsibility on the reader, who must determine whether the information is as reputable as it would be from a traditional news outlet. Some readers might make an educated assessment and weigh the source while determining how to interpret the information. Advocates of traditional media outlets worry that as time passes consumers of news might be less aware of the differences in the type of reporting being done.

Even more, readers may have less access to actual news reports. In the 2009 *State of the News Media* report, researchers note that blogs and Web sites produced by citizen journalists contained a much higher proportion of opinion than actual news stories. The report also found that those news stories that did appear tended to cite fewer sources.

Newspapers have long separated objective news from clearly labeled commentary or editorial pages where opinions are expressed. Television news networks have entire programs devoted to opinionated debates of issues but still have separate news reports. Those who are not journalists but address news on blogs and Tweets do not have the same obligation to report in a fair and accurate way. Twitter and blogs are personal accounts and postings. The risk of such forms is that balanced reporting is replaced by simply commenting on issues.

Traditional Reporting versus Citizen Journalism

As a group, professional reporters tend to have concerns when the work of amateurs is accepted. Issues frequently discussed include:

- Writers who are willing to supply content for free to various emerging Web sites make it more difficult for professionals to receive compensation for their work.
- Untrained writers might not take the use of unnamed sources with the same seriousness as professional writers. This could lead to broken trust of those sources and in turn, less access to those sources.
- Libel laws in relation to the Internet are still being developed and interpreted. Depending on the nature of a site, its writers may not be required to operate within the same set of laws under which journalists operate.

Steve Coll, former *Washington Post* managing editor, said that new additions to the scene do hold promise. He cited technologically savvy Web workers, Internet publishers with the public interest in mind, entrepreneurs, nonprofit organizations entering the marketplace, and an easier access to reporting from around the world as boosts to the greater exchange of information.

Lack of Respect

As the popularity of blogs and Twitter has grown during the first decade of the twenty-first century, their authors and users have defended the medium. One blogger noted:

"The blogosphere as a whole is far greater than the sum of its parts. The constant linkage is its greatest strength and leads the reader direct to the source, or to alternative opinions, or instant responses, or responses to responses. It is the written form of that most basic human interaction: conversation."[8]

Coll said, however, that those boosts cannot offset the loss of professional journalists. In 2008, approximately 16,000 American newspaper workers lost their jobs. Approximately 8,500 more lost their jobs in the first four months of 2009. Coll stated,

> The rate of destruction of professional journalism—and its output of independent reporting on American public institutions and on international affairs—is far outpacing the ability of new institutions to reproduce what is being lost, particularly in its civic functions.[7]

The decline of the newspaper industry has left thousands of trained people looking for work.

WORLD | USA | COMMENTARY | MONEY & VALUES | ENVIRONMENT | INNOVATION

Politics Economy Foreign Policy Justice Military Society & Culture Rebuilding the Econ

Inaugural capstone: The Obamas, Bidens, and Clintons were at Washington National Cathedral Jan. 21 for a prayer service.
CHARLES DHARAPAK/AP

e role of religion under Obama

y's National Prayer Service featured an array of faith leaders, as D
ness and a fuller religious voice.

The Christian Science Monitor *published its final edition on March 26, 2009, before going to a weekly and online-only format.*

STATE OF THE INDUSTRY

Whether one considers the size of the newsroom staff, the size of the product, or circulation numbers, there is no doubt the newspaper industry is shrinking. More than half of the 259 U.S. newspapers surveyed by the

Pew Research Center's Project for Excellence in Journalism reduced their full-time newsroom staffs between 2005 and 2008. Sixty-one percent decreased the amount of space devoted to news during that same time span. The trend increased through 2009.

According to the Project for Excellence in Journalism's 2009 annual report, *The State of the News Media*, "The trends seen in 2008 are signs of serious problems, bad in 2006 and 2007, getting worse in 2009."[1] The findings in the 2009 report include:

Hopeful Sign?

The first half of 2009 was a difficult time for newspapers in the United States. Philadelphia, Pennsylvania, was hit especially hard. That February, the city's two major newspapers—the *Inquirer* and *Daily News*—filed for bankruptcy protection. However, in August 2009, both newspapers filed paperwork in an effort to reorganize and emerge from bankruptcy.

❖ Newspaper circulation was down 4.6 percent for daily newspapers and 4.8 percent for Sunday newspapers during a six-month period in 2007 and 2008. (However, the Newspaper Association of America notes that the number of people turning to newspapers' Web sites continues to grow and topped 70 million in 2009.)

- Newspaper advertising fell by 18 percent in the second half of 2008.

- Newspapers made $49.5 billion in advertising in 2006 and only $38 billion in 2008.

- Viewership remained the same or decreased for most local television news broadcasts in all time slots. Although the viewership increased for cable news, the audience for network news declined somewhat.

- Despite being an election year, when political advertising usually pushes revenue up at television stations, 2008 advertising revenue decreased from that of 2007.[2]

Cutting Costs

In an effort to cut losses, some newspapers intentionally reduced sales to some markets. The *Chicago Tribune* stopped traditional efforts to distribute the newspaper throughout all of Illinois. Many other papers decided to eliminate outlying, and other more costly portions, of their circulation areas. Even though advertising rates at newspapers are based on circulation totals, there were times when it was no

Some newspapers have had to cut sections in order to save money.

longer worth the extra delivery costs to seek relatively small parts of the total sales. Newspapers have to balance the benefits of increased circulation with the costs of delivery. On one hand, higher circulation means they can charge higher rates to advertisers. On the other hand, delivery to some outlying markets can be costly. Newspapers decided the increased revenue from advertising would not offset the delivery costs.

Publishers have taken extreme steps to try to save money and return newspapers to previous profit levels. More newspapers are being printed on smaller-sized pages of thinner, less expensive paper. Many papers have cut content that covers issues outside the market's reach as well as extra sections, such as the business section. Some newspapers, including the *New York Times*, have cut the number of sections printed. Others, such as *The Virginian-Pilot*, have reduced their coverage of outlying areas.

Newspapers have attempted to keep local stories, including investigative pieces, but what defines the "local area" has been reduced. Some newspapers have become "hyper-local." They provide detailed coverage of a specific area, such as an individual neighborhood or block. Other newspapers have begun eliminating staff coverage for state government or regional sports.

When jobs are cut, workers with more experience, who generally have higher salaries, are often eliminated. The younger workers, with lower salaries, have often been the ones who are retained. Typically, the tradeoff means a loss of local experience while improving Web-based reporting. Both print and online products tend to have more errors because the staff has less time and fewer resources to edit the stories.

The Role of Government

The entire news industry, particularly newspapers, entered 2009 in need of a drastic change of course. On May 6, 2009, the U.S. Senate Committee on Commerce, Science, and Transportation held the Hearing on the Future of Journalism to gather information about the crisis.

Unlike the struggling banking and automobile industries, which had received government assistance to try to solve their serious financial woes, news operations had to resist any potential help. Keeping journalism independent from the government prevents politicians from directly influencing the news.

In past decades, regulations involved in issuing radio and television broadcast licenses gave the government some legitimate reasons for being involved in media issues. The government required

Covering Themselves

Sports teams and leagues now produce daily news that looks similar to that produced by independent news outlets. In some cases, the teams and leagues have their own television networks. With media outlets cutting back on their coverage and fewer press credentials being used by traditional sources, team-sponsored and league-sponsored journalists now fill the press box. These broadcasters, reporters, and writers perform many of the same tasks as they did working for news organizations. Meanwhile, the extra seats that used to be reserved for newspaper reporters are sometimes going to new media professionals.

the stations to serve some public interest in order to occupy a frequency. The government put measures in place to avoid monopolies, so that one company was not dominating many media forms. However, many of those restrictions had been eased prior to the crisis that hit U.S. journalism.

Former *Washington Post* managing editor Steve Coll pointed to the broadcast and cross-ownership regulations as an example of the government having some limited involvement in journalism. In testimony at the Future of Journalism hearing, Coll said:

> The rapid and large-scale loss of independent reporting . . . without any prospect of its replacement by new institutions in the foreseeable future, is an urgent matter of public interest. [3]

Coll also said the essential question for the Senate was whether the current journalism crisis was enough of a public interest issue to warrant policy changes. Policy changes might include government subsidies for newspapers. He conceded that such questions include another concern: "whether those reforms can be undertaken without reducing the distance between government and journalism." [4]

An Analysis

The Pew Research Center analyzed the current crisis in depth. Its 2008 study, entitled "The Changing Newsroom," found that newspapers have tended to reduce rather than eliminate areas of coverage. For example, major newspapers have closed many full-time bureaus operating in foreign countries. In a new approach, U.S.-based reporters travel out of the country for specific stories. When beat writers were eliminated from the staff, their beats were often reassigned to a reporter who would be responsible for tracking multiple beats. This could spread a single reporter among a court hearing, a legislative vote, a basketball game,

Questionable Ideas

The search to make money at modern newspapers apparently led to questionable judgment at the *Washington Post* in 2009. A memo from the *Post* had offered lobbyists and executives off-the-record, nonconfrontational access to politicians as well as the newspaper's reporters and editors.

Politico's Mike Allen reported that the meetings in the home of *Post* CEO and publisher Katherine Weymouth were being promoted at prices from $25,000 to $250,000. At issue was whether powerful people should be allowed to buy access to journalists. Journalists, according to their professional codes of ethics, are supposed to maintain their independence.

The meetings were written off as a misunderstanding and never actually happened. *Post* editor Marcus Brauchli, in a memo to the staff, made it clear that the newsroom would not be part of such events.

and a school board meeting, for example. "In interviews, editors of newspapers that had undergone significant newsroom cuts repeatedly found themselves hard-pressed to name beats that had been abandoned completely," the report found. "But they agreed the coverage had become thinner and, because of that quality had diminished."[5]

The study also found that investigative and explanatory journalism projects on major issues were often protected as an essential staple of newspapers. However, coverage on many smaller issues became diluted.

Editors said combining Web work with newspaper work was becoming less of a distraction and that print journalists were learning how to use the Web to break news in ways they could not before.

"I believe there's a very strong place in our society for the printed word," *Lawrence* (Kansas) *Journal-World* editor Dolph C. Simons Jr. said. "It's up to us to find out how best to utilize that opportunity."[6]

As the industry changes, reporters are having to take on more responsibilities, such a taking photos and video.

Some people are looking to the government to help save newspapers.

Financing the Future

Much has already changed in the way news is reported. Dramatic cutbacks have already eliminated many news reporters. With more cutbacks likely, there may be drastically less or different coverage—or both. Certainly, journalists will have to learn to report across multiple media, including print and online platforms.

Exactly how the journalism landscape will change is unknown. The cost-effectiveness and immediacy of the Internet ensures the Web will play a major role. How the people who gather the news will be paid, and how those new journalism ventures will be funded is another question. And only time will tell what becomes of the printed newspaper.

What Does the Future Hold?

During the May 6, 2009, Senate committee hearing on the Future of Journalism, experts shared their visions and opinions about what the future might hold. Arianna Huffington, cofounder and editor-in-chief of one of the most successful blogs, the Huffington Post, spoke of a hybrid model. She said old media and new media could adopt each other's best practices. In her model, old media would take advantage of immediacy and interactivity of new media. Meanwhile, new media could learn more about fairness, accuracy, and investigative journalism.

It is generally agreed that the government and journalism should be kept separate. However, some news organizations and legislators are starting to raise discussion of tax breaks and government incentives for failing newspapers. *Dallas Morning News* publisher and CEO James Moroney requested the Senate consider three steps. He asked for tax relief to help newspapers offset losses from 2008 and 2009. Moroney also requested greater flexibility in allowing newspapers to work together to find alternative business models. His last request was for help ensuring that publishers are fairly

Newspaper Revitalization Act

Benjamin L. Cardin, a Democratic senator from Maryland, sees the newspaper business model as broken. Currently, circulation and advertising revenue pay for the reporting. Cardin proposed the Newspaper Revitalization Act in 2009 as a way to help struggling newspapers be transformed into nonprofit organizations.

Cardin sees saving newspapers as essential, despite the other emerging media outlets. In a piece for a *Washington Post* Op-Ed, he wrote:

My goal is to save local coverage by reporters who know their communities, work their beats and dig up the stories that are important to our daily lives. Today newspapers do that job; all other outlets—TV, radio, blogs—feed off that base. The bill would allow newspapers—if they choose—to operate under 501(c)(3) status for educational purposes, similar to public broadcasters.[1]

Cardin proposed limitations that would assure such nonprofit status is not misused. "Under this arrangement, newspapers would not be allowed to make political endorsements but would be permitted to freely report on all issues, including political campaigns. . . . Newspapers provide a vital service," Cardin said. "It is in the interest of our nation and good governance that we ensure their survival."[2]

paid or compensated for content picked up by others on the Web. Moroney suggested publishers be paid when search engines and news aggregators pick up breaking news.

New Laws?

The Federal Communications Commission (FCC) banned owners in a given media market from owning both a newspaper and a broadcast station in 1975. Those laws were put in place to prevent companies from using unfair business practices to dominate the market and make unfair profits. In 2007, the FCC voted to allow cross-ownership in the same market. However, in 2008, the Senate voted to throw out that ruling.

Alberto Ibarguen, president of the John S. and James L. Knight Foundation, said laws related to the industry are outdated. He said changes could "extend the usefulness" of newspapers and broadcast stations by making it easier for them to work together. "At the time those laws were passed, the people's interest lay in preventing the concentration of power and to encourage a democratic diversity of voices," Ibarguen said. "One might question whether . . . this is still a valid concern and whether the bankruptcy of a news organization that is not allowed to merge to survive serves the democracy."[3]

A Continued Evolution

Current trends suggest that more and more information will be shared through digital access as well as mobile devices. E-mail and full Internet access have become common through cell phones. Some consumers sign up for news alerts that can be delivered to their cell phones.

Huffington said that choosing sides between old and new media would not be helpful. She told the Senate, "The answer can't be content creators attacking Google and other news [collectors]." She also said, "It's important to remember that the future of quality journalism is not dependent on the future of newspapers."[4]

Some are worried about losing journalism professionals through the newspaper cutbacks. But Huffington sees the positives in the new options available. "Journalism will not only survive, it will thrive," she said. "Despite all the hand wringing about the dire state of the newspaper industry . . . we are actually in the midst of a Golden Age for news consumers."[5]

Not everyone is convinced. Where Huffington sees Web surfing, search engines, and news aggregators providing countless options for news coverage, others see fewer professionals doing the original reporting. "In this new evolving world, trusted sources, adhering to fact-checking mores of traditional journalism, are often too few and far between," said Senator John D. Rockefeller IV, a Democrat from West Virginia and chairman of the Science, Commerce and Transportation Committee. "The important and time-consuming work of investigative reporting may lack the institutional support it needs to thrive."[6]

Equal Access

Alberto Ibarguen is the president of the charitable John S. and James L. Knight Foundation. He suggested one way the government could be involved in protecting journalism without becoming too closely aligned.

Noting the increased frequency with which the public receives information through the Internet, Ibarguen urged a Senate subcommittee on the future of journalism to make sure every American has digital access. As the Internet has grown, higher speed connections to the available information have become more necessary.

Many fear less reporting means simple repetition of the same information in different forms. They also worry about the weakening role of watchdog journalism. Benjamin L. Cardin, a Democratic senator from Maryland, wrote a 2009 Op-Ed piece in the *Washington Post*. He asked people not to forget the role newspapers played in uncovering scandals such as Watergate. He noted that newspapers have also played a major role in uncovering corruption and questionable practices at major U.S. corporations such as Enron and AIG.

Getting the Message Out

Businesses and public entities unhappy with the way they are covered by the media can use Web sites to deliver their own messages. When television news budgets shrunk, savvy special interest groups and businesses stepped in. They produced articles that looked like news reports and succeeded in getting them on the air without always being labeled as promotional items. Rather than simply making sales pitches, more organizations are hiring professional writers to produce content for their Web sites. Although the content takes the form of news stories, it promotes a product or an idea.

The New Plan

If newspapers cannot remain viable, then the future media need to find ways to earn money so they can pay news gatherers. Some argue that a democracy can move forward without print media. Still, others such as Cardin argue that only newspapers deliver the kind of active, investigative journalism that provides important checks and balances of government and other public institutions. He said:

> While the world has increasingly fast access to news, one fact remains unchanged: When it comes to original, in-depth reporting that records and exposes actions, issues,

and opportunities in our communities, nothing has replaced newspapers. Most, if not all, sources of journalistic information, from Google to broadcast news or punditry, gain their original material from the laborious and expensive work of experienced newspaper reporters diligently working their beats over the course of years. Not hours, years.[7]

Cardin has proposed tax breaks that would make it easier for newspapers to switch to a nonprofit status if they chose to do so. But skeptics of such proposals wonder if it is possible to get enough donations to fund a nonprofit organization without introducing new influences that are supposed to be kept separate from journalism. In other words, can a nonprofit funded by donations still produce unbiased reporting?

If the solution is not determined quickly enough, news operations could lose their audience as their product becomes less informative. Lost readers and viewers might not be easily regained if and when a new model for producing news is found. From television news programs to newspapers, media outlets have thrived when their strong reputations have made them a daily necessity for their consumers.

In order to make journalism a successful business, as opposed to the nonprofit model, news operations must be funded. For decades, advertising paid for the work print journalists produced. Advertising, including that garnered from entertainment programming, also funded broadcast news operations. Of course, in the past some critics feared advertising could influence reporting as well.

Another potential revenue source is readers who pay for the product. However, this option presents its own challenges. The vast amount of free information available online has made it difficult for media entities to charge for their online content. Still, many argue that news organizations should stop giving away their content. One suggestion is that the government could limit the ability of others to use the work of professional journalists without paying for it. Another is that the government could allow groups of competing newspapers to team together. By teaming up, newspapers would have more control over who reads their content and how it spreads online. Currently, such a level of control would violate antitrust laws. Such laws are meant to discourage monopolies while allowing smaller news organizations a chance to compete.

Allowing broadcast stations and newspapers more flexibility to work with each other could benefit both media.

Complicating matters is that the media is considering trying to sell what it has offered for free. Consumers are not used to having to pay for news online. Also, all online newspapers would have to act in unison. For example, if the *Washington Post* gives away stories on the Internet, it becomes even more difficult for the *New York Times* to sell similar information.

Journalists once lived by the ideal that they should keep themselves completely separate from the industry's business issues. This model of separation supposedly resulted in less biased reporting. It is now more common for journalists, especially editorial managers, to consider ways of generating income from the work they produce. Coverage can become unbalanced if a reporter or an editor knows one type of information will sell better than another, even if the less marketable information may have larger social or political impacts.

News of the Future

The question of whether print newspapers should be or can be salvaged remains unanswered. And steering the evolution of news reporting in a productive and socially beneficial direction will likely require many approaches. Senator Rockefeller is hopeful that regardless of the medium in which it is delivered, good journalism will become a foundation of the nation's future. "We are undoubtedly in a transformational period for the news-gathering business," he said. "Though the challenges before us are many, sustaining quality journalism is a cause that is worth the fight."[8]

The future of news reporting is likely to be largely online.

TIMELINE

ca. 60 BCE

Roman Emperor
Julius Caesar orders
the posting of a
daily sheet of events
throughout Rome.

ca. 700s

Variations of
newspapers
appear in China.

1690

Publick Occurrences,
the first North
American newspaper,
appears in Boston.

1791

Freedom of the
press is assured
importance in the
United States when
Congress ratifies
the Bill of Rights.

ca. 1440

Johannes Gutenberg creates the modern movable type printing press in Germany.

late 1400s

News pamphlets, or broadsides, appear in Germany.

ca. 1600s

The *Oxford/London Gazette* utilizes double columns and evolves into what is considered the first true newspaper.

1940

CBS begins *The World Today* program, the first regular radio broadcast of daily news.

1963

On September 2, the *CBS Evening News* becomes the first nightly network news to expand to 30 minutes.

TIMELINE

1968

CBS begins the *60 Minutes* weekly news magazine show.

1969

The first message is sent over ARPANET, the predecessor of the Internet.

2006

Twitter is founded, allowing millions of people to instantly share messages.

2007

The FCC votes to allow cross-ownership of newspapers with broadcast stations in the same market.

1974

The *Washington Post* links President Nixon's administration to the Watergate scandal, eventually leading to Nixon's resignation.

1980

Ted Turner creates the Cable News Network (CNN), which broadcasts news 24 hours a day, seven days a week.

1994

Netscape releases the first commercially available Web browser.

2008

The Senate votes to throw out the FCC's 2007 ruling, which would have ended the ban on cross-ownership.

2009

On February 27, the *Rocky Mountain News* prints its final edition.

2009

On May 6, the U.S. Senate holds the Hearing on the Future of Journalism.

Essential Facts

At Issue

❖ Many believe that using public funds to aid an ailing industry would remove the separation of government and media that is essential to a democracy.

❖ As technology continues to change, print newspapers continue to lose readership to online sources.

❖ Web sites, including blogs and sites that feature "citizen journalism," have provided some alternative options to traditional news sources.

❖ The loss of jobs for trained journalists eliminates many of the "watchdogs" that help monitor government agencies and other businesses in roles that impact society.

❖ Amateurs, who are not trained in proper journalistic methods, produce some of the online news content. They do not always understand the journalistic principles of verifying information with multiple sources and keeping their own opinions out of stories.

❖ Access to free news on the Internet has damaged established news operations, particularly for newspapers.

❖ Newspaper companies around the country are drastically reducing their staffs, which decreases the amount of reporting being done on issues that affect the public. Some newspapers have stopped publishing, and others have sought bankruptcy protection.

❖ The Federal Communications Commission (FCC) banned cross-ownership of newspapers and broadcast stations in the same market in 1975 to try to control the possibility of media monopolies.

❖ The Newspaper Revitalization Act was proposed in 2009 as a potential way to give tax breaks to struggling newspapers that wanted to sell to or become nonprofit organizations.

CRITICAL DATES

1974
Richard Nixon became the only U.S. president to resign. Reporters Bob Woodward and Carl Bernstein had linked the White House to Watergate break-ins in a series of *Washington Post* news reports.

2009
The *Rocky Mountain News*, Colorado's oldest newspaper, published its last edition. The Denver newspaper shut down just before what would have been its 150th anniversary. The U.S. Senate Committee on Commerce, Science, and Transportation heard testimony from several industry experts during a hearing on the future of journalism.

QUOTES

"Were it left to me to decide whether we should have a government without newspapers, or newspapers without a government, I should not hesitate a moment to prefer the latter."—*Thomas Jefferson, third president of the United States*

"It's important to remember that the future of quality journalism is not dependent on the future of newspapers."—*Arianna Huffington, cofounder and editor in chief of the Huffington Post*

ADDITIONAL RESOURCES

SELECT BIBLIOGRAPHY

Burgh, Hugo de. *Investigative Journalism: Context and Practice*. New York, NY: Routledge, 2000.

"The Changing Newsroom." *Journalism.org*. 21 July 2008. 10 Sept. 2009 <http://www.journalism.org/node/11961>.

"The Presence of Magazines on the Internet." *The Bivings Report*. 29 Nov. 2006. 10 Sept. 2009 <http://www.bivingsreport.com/2006/the-presence-of-magazines-on-the-internet/>.

"The Use of the Internet by America's Newspapers." *The Bivings Report*. 1 Aug. 2006. 10 Sept. 2009 <http://www.bivingsreport.com/campaign/newspapers06_tz-fgb.pdf>.

FURTHER READING

Schaffer, James, Randall McCutcheon, and Kathryn T. Stofer. *Journalism Matters*. Lincolnwood, IL: National Textbook Co., 2001.

Smith, Erica. "Paper Cuts." <http://graphicdesignr.net/papercuts>.

United States. Cong. Senate. Committee on Commerce, Science, and Transportation. *Hearing on The Future of Journalism.* 111th Cong., 1st sess. Washington. 6 May 2009 <http://commerce.senate.gov/public/index.cfm?p=Hearings&ContentRecord_id=7f8df1a5-5504-4f4c-ba34-ba3dc3955c61&ContentType_id=14f995b9-dfa5-407a-9d35-56cc7152a7ed&Group_id=b06c39af-e033-4cba-9221-de668ca1978a&MonthDisplay=5&YearDisplay=2009>.

WEB LINKS

To learn more about the evolution of news reporting, visit ABDO Publishing Company on the World Wide Web at **www.abdopublishing.com**. Web sites about news reporting are featured on our Book Links page. These links are routinely monitored and updated to provide the most current information available.

For More Information

For more information on this subject, contact or visit the following organizations.

Franklin Court
316-322 Market Street, Philadelphia, PA 19106
267-519-4295
www.ushistory.org/tour/tour_fcourt.htm
Benjamin Franklin is remembered at the Franklin Print Shop and Franklin Museum. View printing demonstrations at the printing office and bindery and a restored office of *The Aurora and General Advertiser*, a newspaper published by Franklin's grandson, Benjamin Franklin Bache.

The Museum of Broadcast Communications
676 North LaSalle Street, Suite 424, Chicago, IL 60654
312-245-8200
www.museum.tv
The museum collects, preserves, and presents historic and contemporary radio and television content. It offers access to its archives, public programs, screenings, exhibitions, and publications.

Newseum
555 Pennsylvania Avenue Northwest, Washington, DC 20001
888-639-7386
www.newseum.org
The museum offers visitors a blend of five centuries of news history and hands-on exhibits featuring the latest technology. The museum has seven levels, which include galleries, theaters, retail spaces, and visitor services.

Glossary

aggregator
> The software or Web site that collects headlines and links from other sources to form a news report.

beat
> An area of concentration for a news reporter such as city government, education, health, or a local sports team.

blog
> A Web site that posts a series of entries on a topic in order from newest to oldest. A blog, or Weblog, often links to material from other Web sites or sources.

blogger
> A person who writes or compiles information on a blog.

browsing
> The process of navigating from one Web site to another; also known as surfing.

circulation
> The number of copies a newspaper distributes. Paid circulation is the number of newspapers sold.

copyright
> The legal rights given exclusively to the creator or owner of a work, allowing him or her to publish the work.

libel
> A false statement about a person, spread through print or through broadcast, that injures the person's reputation or standing in the community.

newsprint

Thin, inexpensive paper used for printing newspapers.

Op-Ed

Opinion and editorial columns and pages in a newspaper, which are generally separated from news.

public relations

Promotional work intended to create a positive public image and to ensure that an organization's viewpoints are communicated to various audiences.

stock market

A market for the public trading of stock in companies.

surfing

The process of navigating from one Web site to another; also known as browsing.

Tweet

To post a text message on the Twitter.com Web site.

Twitter

A Web site that connects members who post a series of brief messages.

unions

Groups of people who work together toward a common purpose.

watchdog

A nickname for a journalist responsible for providing information the public should be aware of. A watchdog "barks" when powers that be take questionable actions.

SOURCE NOTES

Chapter 1. The Financial Crunch

1. Tim Reese. "Rocky Mountain News Closes." *The Frame.* Sacramento Bee. 26 Feb. 2009. 22 July 2009 <http://www.sacbee.com/static/weblogs/ photos/2009/02/020125.html>.

2. "Rocky Mountain Closes—Friday Final Edition." *Rocky Mountain News.* 26 Feb. 2009. 7 June 2009 <http://www.rockymountainnews.com/ news/2009/feb/26/rocky-mountain-news-closes-friday-final-edition/>.

3. Ibid.

4. Michael F. Bennet. "Sen. Bennet's Statement on Closing of Rocky Mountain News." *Michael F. Bennet United States Senator for Colorado.* 26 Feb. 2009. 1 Sept. 2009 <http://bennet.senate.gov/newsroom/floor_ statements/statements/?id=b0d91285-63f7-4807-8fa9-663111111a62>.

5. Clay Shirky. "Newspapers and Thinking the Unthinkable." *Clay Shirky's Writings About the Internet.* 13 Mar. 2009. 7 June 2009 <http://www.shirky. com/weblog/2009/03/newspapers-and-thinking-the-unthinkable/>.

Chapter 2. The Birth of the News Industry

1. "United States Constitution." *Cornell University Law School.* 1 Sept. 2009 <http://www.law.cornell.edu/constitution/constitution.billofrights. html>.

2. "Thomas Jefferson on Politics and Government." *University of Virginia.* 22 July 2009 <http://etext.virginia.edu/jefferson/quotations/jeff1600.htm>.

3. Eric Alterman. "Out of Print." *New Yorker.* 31 Mar. 2008. 7 June 2009 <http://www.newyorker.com/reporting/2008/03/31/080331fa_fact_ alterman?currentPage=all>.

Chapter 3. The Impact of the Internet

1. Eugene Robinson. "Boston Globe and Other Papers Struggle to Survive." *Washington Post.* 5 May 2009. 14 July 2009 <http://www. washingtonpost.com/wp-dyn/content/discussion/2009/05/01/ DI2009050102592.html>.

2. Stephen Brook. "News reporting faces web challenge, warns New York Times editor." *Guardian.* 29 Nov. 2007. 14 July 2009 <http://www. guardian.co.uk/media/2007/nov/29/pressandpublishing.digitalmedia>.

3. Ibid.

Chapter 4. Struggles with Technology and Copyright

1. Clay Shirky. "Newspapers and Thinking the Unthinkable." *Clay Shirky's Writings About the Internet.* 13 Mar. 2009. 7 June 2009 <http://www.shirky. com/weblog/2009/03/newspapers-and-thinking-the-unthinkable/>.

2. Ibid.

3. "AP Board announces initiative to protect industry's content; Further rate reductions and new 'Limited' service respond to member needs." *Associated Press.* 6 Apr. 2009. 27 Aug. 2009 <http://www.ap.org/pages/about/pressreleases/pr_040609a.html>.

Chapter 5. The News of Today

1. Scott Collins and Greg Braxton. "TV misses out as gossip website TMZ reports Michael Jackson's death first." *Los Angeles Times.* 26 June 2009.
2. Ibid.
3. United States. Cong. Senate. Committee on Commerce, Science, and Transportation. *Hearing on The Future of Journalism.* 111th Cong., 1st sess. Washington. 6 May 2009. 20 July 2009 < http://commerce.senate.gov/public/?a=Files.Serve&File_id=c7c8ec36-51e2-4163-889f-36b777f6a771>.
4. Scott Spjut. "Journalism: The End or the Beginning?" *Demockracy.com.* 11 May 2009. 9 Sept. 2009 <http://demockracy.com/journalism-the-end-or-the-beginning/>.
5. Ibid.
6. United States. Cong. Senate. Committee on Commerce, Science, and Transportation. *Hearing on The Future of Journalism.* 111th Cong., 1st sess. Washington. 6 May 2009. 20 July 2009 < http://commerce.senate.gov/public/?a=Files.Serve&File_id=9392d321-43e8-4053-bdbb-466070864d5e>.
7. Ibid.
8. Ibid.

Chapter 6. Media as a Watchdog

1. Barry Sussman. "About Us: Why Watchdog? And Why Questions?" *Nieman Watchdog.* 15 Sept. 2009. <www.niemanwatchdog.org/index.cfm?fuseaction=about.Mission_Statement>.
2. Anne E. Kornblut. "The News Media Is Still Recovering From Watergate." *New York Times.* 5 June 2005. 17 Sept. 2009 <http://www.nytimes.com/2005/06/05/weekinreview/05korn.html>.
3. Ibid.
4. United States. Cong. Senate. Committee on Commerce, Science, and Transportation. *Hearing on The Future of Journalism.* 111th Cong., 1st sess. Washington. 6 May 2009. 20 July 2009 < http://commerce.senate.gov/public/?a=Files.Serve&File_id=9392d321-43e8-4053-bdbb-466070864d5e>.

Source Notes Continued

5. Anne E. Kornblut. "The News Media Is Still Recovering From Watergate." *New York Times.* 5 June 2005. 17 Sept. 2009 <http://www.nytimes.com/2005/06/05/weekinreview/05korn.html>.
6. United States. Cong. Senate. Committee on Commerce, Science, and Transportation. *Hearing on The Future of Journalism.* 111th Cong., 1st sess. Washington. 6 May 2009. 20 July 2009 < http://commerce.senate.gov/public/?a=Files.Serve&File_id=0330b270-52b7-4938-9d81-c55318a4194d>.

Chapter 7. A Different Style
1. "Hey there! OneSimpleAct is using twitter." Twitter. n.d. 17 Sept. 2009 <http://twitter.com/OneSimpleAct>.
2. Josephine Cusumano. "All a-Twitter." *unbound.* n.d. 17 Sept. 2009 <http://www.tcnj.edu/~unbound/article.php?id=907>
3. Eric Zeman. "Twitter Spreads News of U.S. Airways Crash In An Instant." *Informationweek.com.* 15 June 2009. 20 July 2009 <http://www.informationweek.com/blog/main/archives/2009/01/twitter_spreads.html;jsessionid=EKTGWLIRIRLNMQSNDLOSKH0CJUNN2JVN>.
4. Ibid.
5. "Top 100 Twitterholics based on Followers." *Twitterholic.com.* April 2010. 6 April. 2010 <http://twitterholic.com>.
6. "Top 25 Most Popular Blogs." *eBizMBA.com.* July 2009. 20 July 2009 <http://www.ebizmba.com/articles/blogs>.
7. United States. Cong. Senate. Committee on Commerce, Science, and Transportation. *Hearing on The Future of Journalism.* 111th Cong., 1st sess. Washington. 6 May 2009. 20 July 2009 < http://commerce.senate.gov/public/?a=Files.Serve&File_id=0330b270-52b7-4938-9d81-c55318a4194d>.
8. Simon. "In Defence of Blogging." *Showcase.* 28 June 2004. 6 Apr. 2010 < http://showcase.mu.nu/archives/033671.php>.

Chapter 8. State of the Industry
1. "The State of the News Media 2009." *Journalism.org.* 27 Aug. 2009 <http://www.stateofthemedia.org/2009/narrative_newspapers_intro.php?cat=0&media=4>.
2. Ibid.
3. United States. Cong. Senate. Committee on Commerce, Science, and Transportation. *Hearing on The Future of Journalism.* 111th Cong., 1st sess. Washington. 6 May 2009. 20 July 2009 < http://commerce.senate.gov/public/?a=Files.Serve&File_id=0330b270-52b7-4938-9d81-c55318a4194d>.

4. Ibid.

5. "The Changing Newsroom: Changing Content." *Journalism.org*. 21 July 2008. 20 July 2009 <http://www.journalism.org/node/11963>.

6. "The Changing Newsroom: Conclusion." Journalism.org. 21 July 2008. 20 July 2009 <http://www.journalism.org/node/11979>.

Chapter 9. Financing the Future

1. Benjamin L. Cardin. "A Plan to Save Our Free Press." *Washington Post*. 3 Apr. 2009. 22 July 2009 <http://www.washingtonpost.com/wp-dyn/content/article/2009/04/02/AR2009040203310.html>.

2. Ibid.

3. Alberto Ibarguen. "Hearing on the Future of Journalism." 6 May 2009. 20 July 2009 <http://commerce.senate.gov/public/_files/AlbertoIbarguenFutureofJournalismTestimony.pdf>.

4. United States. Cong. Senate. Committee on Commerce, Science, and Transportation. *Hearing on The Future of Journalism*. 111th Cong., 1st sess. Washington. 6 May 2009. 20 July 2009 < http://commerce.senate.gov/public/?a=Files.Serve&File_id=ba1909cf-1f10-4654-81e0-d3e9cc254743>.

5. Ibid.

6. United States. Cong. Senate. Committee on Commerce, Science, and Transportation. *Hearing on The Future of Journalism*. 111th Cong., 1st sess. Washington. 6 May 2009. 20 July 2009 < http://commerce.senate.gov/public/index.cfm?p=Hearings&ContentRecord_id=7f8df1a5-5504-4f4c-ba34-ba3dc3955c61&Statement_id=b5050fd1-75aa-45cb-83f0-c5793901cd07&ContentType_id=14f995b9-dfa5-407a-9d35-56cc7152a7ed&Group_id=b06c39af-e033-4cba-9221-de668ca1978a&MonthDisplay=5&YearDisplay=2009>.

7. Benjamin L. Cardin. "A Plan to Save Our Free Press." *Washington Post*. 3 Apr. 2009. 22 July 2009 <http://www.washingtonpost.com/wp-dyn/content/article/2009/04/02/AR2009040203310.html>.

8. United States. Cong. Senate. Committee on Commerce, Science, and Transportation. *Hearing on The Future of Journalism*. 111th Cong., 1st sess. Washington. 6 May 2009. 20 July 2009 < http://commerce.senate.gov/public/index.cfm?p=Hearings&ContentRecord_id=7f8df1a5-5504-4f4c-ba34-ba3dc3955c61&Statement_id=b5050fd1-75aa-45cb-83f0-c5793901cd07&ContentType_id=14f995b9-dfa5-407a-9d35-56cc7152a7ed&Group_id=b06c39af-e033-4cba-9221-de668ca1978a&MonthDisplay=5&YearDisplay=2009>.

INDEX

ABOUT THE AUTHOR

Tom Robinson spent 17 years as an editor, writer, and statistician for daily newspapers. Since becoming a freelance writer and editor, he has written more than 20 books for young readers. Robinson's report on the use of expense money within the Pennsylvania Interscholastic Athletic Association (PIAA) was selected as one of the top ten news stories in the 50,000–175,000 circulation category in 1998 by the Associated Press Sports Editors. He also received media awards from two districts of the PIAA. He lives in Pennsylvania with his family.

PHOTO CREDITS

Mario Tama/Getty Images, cover, 3; David Zalubowski/AP Images, 6, 11, 99 (bottom); AP Images, 15, 30, 58, 65, 68, 98, 99 (top); North Wind Picture Archives/Photolibrary, 16, 97 (top); Eliza Snow/iStockphoto, 19, 96; Arne Thaysen/iStockphoto, 25; Dmitriy Shironosov/iStockphoto, 26; Getty Images, 33; Chris Schmidt/iStockphoto, 37; Joseph Kaczmarek/AP Images, 38; iStockphoto, 42, 83, 84, 93, 97 (bottom); Big Stock Photo, 47, 77; Jeff Widerner/AP Images, 48; Gareth Cattermole/Getty Images, 51; Bart Sadowski/iStockphoto, 57; Reed Saxon/AP Images, 61; Bebeto Matthews/AP Images, 66; Rick Bowmer/AP Images, 73; Michael Dwyer/AP Images, 74; Izabela Habur/iStockphoto, 95